Techniques of
SAFECRACKING

Wayne B. Yeager

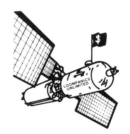

Loompanics Unlimited
Port Townsend, Washington

This book is sold for information purposes only. Neither the author nor the publisher will be held accountable for the use or misuse of the information contained in this book.

TECHNIQUES OF SAFECRACKING
© 1990 by Wayne B. Yeager

Published by:
Loompanics Unlimited
P.O. Box 1197
Port Townsend, WA 98368
Loompanics Unlimited is a division of Loompanics Enterprises, Inc.

Cover & illustrations by Kevin Martin.

ISBN 1-55950-052-2

Library of Congress Catalog Card Number 90-063304

Contents

Introduction

A constant technological war exists between safe-makers and safecrackers. To construct a safe or vault strong enough to keep burglars out, but functional enough to let authorized personnel in, has been the ultimate goal for the manufacturers of safes and vaults since their invention. The race towards this ideal safe has caused frustration for those on both sides of the law in their attempts to defeat the technology of the other. And while neither side may ever ultimately triumph, they both win their share of battles.

The most powerful weapon in the safe manufacturer's arsenal is his ability to attack the burglar on one or more fronts: denying initial access to the safe, strengthening the safe itself, alarming the safe, etc. But the burglar is not completely defenseless either, for he knows a safe can never really be made absolutely foolproof. Why? Because a locksmith or other authority must always be able to enter a safe in case the combination mechanism malfunctions. In other words, while a safe can offer a reasonable amount of protection, it can never be made, out of practical necessity, indestructible. Another problem that facilitates the safecracker's operation is that of obsolescence in safe technology. By the time an anti-burglary device is designed, patented, manufactured, marketed, and made commercially available, professional safecrackers have been experimenting and working to defeat it. The question is not *if* a safety device *can* be bypassed, but rather *when* the device *will* be bypassed.

When one buys a safe, what one is really buying is time. If the safe is on the lower end of the price scale, it can only be expected to resist attack for a short length of time, and if the burglar is using only basic tools and basic knowledge, the safe will more than likely do its job. But as the potential reward inside the safe increases, so does the risk, and so, too, must the protection. This very simple and obvious maxim is often overlooked by homeowners and businessmen. I could not count the number of times I've seen a $200 fire safe holding thousands of dollars in cash, or an 1890 safe expected to withstand 1990 attacks.

This book lists and explains just about all of the methods that are used by both locksmith and safecracker to open safes, vaults, and safe deposit boxes. These techniques range from "soft" openings, such as combination deduction and manipulation, to "hard" openings, such as the application of nitroglycerine or C-4. While some of these techniques may be obsolete on some of the newer, high-tech safes, many will be overkill on the older or less sophisticated models. I've not tried to identify what is obsolete and what is unnecessary, but I do note throughout the text on what models each technique is most often applied.

Safecracking is a crime that has been with us and will be with us for many, many years. I subscribe to the theory that you can't solve a problem unless the problem is fully understood. This book, like my others, is a textbook on crime, a guide so that the security and law-enforcement community may more accurately understand what they're up against. If you are a security consultant, use this guide to more accurately recommend equipment for your client's needs. Police and private investigators will discover invaluable information here for conducting a safecracking investigation. And although this book is written for individuals with no previous locksmithing experience, I believe even the most seasoned safemen will find several new safe-entry tricks here.

1
Safe Mechanics and Operation

Despite the multitude of safes on the market today, they all cling to a basic theory of operation: the protection of contents from outside forces (such as fire and burglary), while allowing authorized entry via a combinational dial, key, or keypad. Safes differ from model to model in the way they accomplish this task, but this is, nevertheless, the basic premise of each. There are two basic types of safes: fire safes, which are insulated to protect important documents from extreme temperatures, and money chests, which are specially designed for extra security, to withstand attacks from determined burglars. Actually, these are overlapping categories, for most fire safes offer some burglary protection, and money chests are protected from small fires as well.

In order to discuss safes intelligibly, we must make ourselves familiar with the basic terms regarding the operation of the typical safe. Figure 1-1 shows an example of the Diebold brand safe. It is essentially a five-walled seamless steel box with an attached door. The door is very thick, with hardened steel plates, and is attached to the box with very strong hinges and a steel deadbolt.

Figure 1-1

This Diebold brand safe is a five-walled seamless steel box with a door attached with very strong hinges and a deadbolt. The door is very thick, containing hardened steel plates.

The safe is opened legitimately by dialing the proper combination on the dial, and turning the handle to release the bolt from the safebox; the door is then free to open. This is a deceptively simple operation, for much more occurs within the walls of the safe, hidden from view.

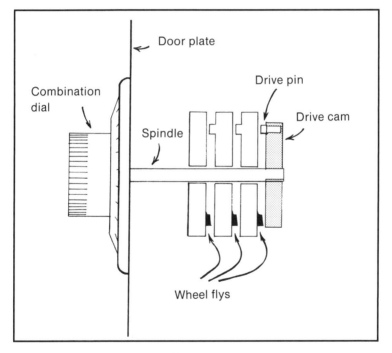

Figure 1-2

The wheel-pack is the mechanical device that "knows" the proper combination has been dialed. Located behind the combination dial, the wheel-pack consists of wheels (usually three or four but sometimes more) that are moved about by turning the dial.

Behind the combination dial is the "wheel-pack," the mechanical device that "knows" when the proper combination has been dialed. The wheel-pack usually consists of three or four wheels (depending on the amount of numbers in the combination sequence, so a 10-20-30 combination will require three wheels) and they are moved about by turning the dial (see Figure 1-2). The combination dial is attached by the spindle to the drive cam. If the dial is turned, the drive pin on the drive cam comes into contact with the fly on the wheel adjacent to it, and that wheel begins turning also. If the combination dial continues to turn, the fly on the first wheel comes into contact with the fly on the next wheel, and so on, until the turning of the combination dial turns all of the wheels in the wheel-pack simultaneously.

Into each of the wheels of the wheel-pack, a deep notch is cut. When the proper combination is dialed, all of these notches in the wheels are aligned perfectly. Just above the wheel-pack is a device known as a gate and fence. As long as the correct combination has not been dialed, the notches will not all be in perfect alignment, and the gate and fence will merely rest upon the wheels (see Figure 1-3). But when the right combination is executed, the wheels align accordingly, and both the gate and fence are allowed to fall into the groove formed by the aligned notches (see Figure 1-4). The lever and fence which were guarding the bolt are now out of the way, and if the handle is turned, the bolt is retracted, and the door opens. If this procedure seems a bit complicated, study the diagrams until you understand this completely.

The lever/bolt mechanism varies slightly from safe to safe. Some are gravity activated, as in our example, but they may be friction or spring-loaded. This is of no consequence, however, for they all act pretty much the same, and the slight differences do not alter the safecracker's methods in the least. The only thing worth noting here is the fact that spring-loaded fence/bolt mechanisms do away with the need for outside handles, since the combination dial retracts the bolt (after the combination has been dialed, of course). This is the type used almost exclusively on round-door safes.

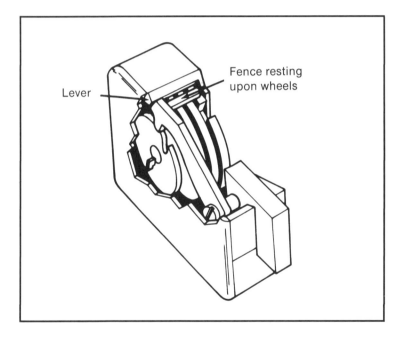

Figure 1-3

If the correct combination has not been dialed, the notches in the wheel-pack will not be aligned, and the gate and fence will merely rest upon the wheels.

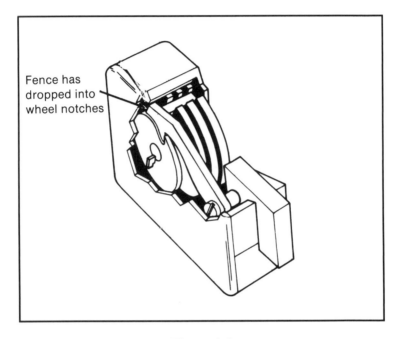

Fence has dropped into wheel notches

Figure 1-4

*When the right combination is dialed, the wheels align,
the gate and fence fall into the right notches.*

When one is dealing with safes, it helps to know all one can about the particular model that is encountered. Underwriters' Laboratories has facilitated this procedure by labeling most safes with a universal code. On the safe body, a small metal tag (see Figure 1-5) will be displayed telling the amount of protection one may expect from fire or burglary. In other words, a burglar in the know can judge by the UL tag just how the safe is protected, and what techniques will or will not work. Handy, huh? Although the people at UL have coded this information slightly, every safecracker worth his salt knows exactly what each identifying code means. Figure 1-6 is a chart of the various codes currently in use.

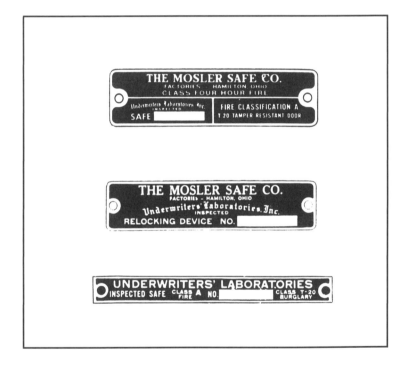

Figure 1-5

Most safes display a small metal tag which contains a coded rating from Underwriters' Laboratories indicating the amount of protection from fire or burglary the safe can be expected to provide. Above are three such tags.

Any other specifics of safe operation will be discussed more thoroughly whenever that information is needed to clarify a certain procedure. You have now, however, all the information you need to understand the next chapter.

UNDERWRITERS' LABORATORY CODES CHART

	Common tools: hammers, chisels, screwdrivers	Jack hammers and impact drills	Power saws and cutting wheels	Oxy-acetylene torches (thermic lances not tested)	High explosives
TL-15 — limited protection from burglary by common tools. Test time: 15 min Test area: door only	Yes	No	No	No	No
TL-30 — moderate protection from expert burglary by common tools. Test time: 30 min Test area: door only	Yes	No	Yes	No	No
TRTL-30 — moderate protection from expert burglary by common tools and cutting torches. Test time: 30 min Test area: door only	Yes	No	Yes	Yes	No
TRTL-30 (x6) — moderate protection against expert burglary by common tools and cutting torches. Test time: 30 min Test area: door and body	Yes	Yes	Yes	Yes	No
TRTL-60 — high degree of protection against expert burglary with common tools, cutting torches. Test time: 60 min Test area: door and body	Yes	Yes	Yes	Yes	No
TXTL-60 — high degree of protection against expert burglary with common tools, cutting torches, and high explosives. Test time: 60 min Test area: door and body	Yes	Yes	Yes	Yes	Yes

Figure 1-6

This chart explains the meaning of various Underwriters' Laboratories safe codes currently in use.

2

Combination Deduction

Since the most convenient way to open a safe is to dial out the proper combination, this chapter deals with how one may go about procuring it. Besides the obvious brute tactics, such as beating it out of someone who knows it, or threatening to do so, there are several tricks burglars use to come by this elusive combination. One of the most successful ways, manipulation, requires in-depth explanation, so the next chapter is devoted exclusively to it. Another method is by using try-out combinations. These combinations are set on the safes by the manufacturers, and are intended to be changed by the new owners, although many people don't know this or are too lazy to bother. Some examples of try-out combinations are in Appendix A, and these will open a surprising number of safes in use today.

A locksmith I know was called upon to open a safe whose owner had just died. The locksmith walked around the room for a few minutes before sitting down in front of the safe. To the family's amazement, the locksmith dialed out the combination and opened the safe in ten seconds flat. Magic? No, my locksmith friend simply realized that most people have terrible memories for numbers, and almost invariably write the combination down somewhere near the safe. He had found it written on the wall by a window, two feet away. I've found combinations written on desks, door frames, window panes, walls, picture frames, telephones, and even on the safe itself! This tendency is so universal, burglars almost always allot a few minutes to combination-hunting before moving on to more extreme measures.

Similarly, due to fallible memory, people have a propensity for making combinations out of notable numbers in their life. For example, I've seen a man whose birthday is October 12, 1931 use 10-12-31 for the combination to his safe. I've also known people to use anniversary dates, parts of Social Security numbers, Armed Forces serial numbers, and birthdates of children and spouses. Next to writing the combination down, this is the favorite method of combination retrieval, and you can bet professional burglars are well aware of it. Many safecrackers will undoubtedly do research to uncover such numbers prior to a house-breaking.

If the above techniques are impossible, the burglar may then try to determine whether or not the owner has left the safe on what is known as "day-lock." Day-lock means that the safe door was closed, and the combination dial was turned slightly. This scrambles only the last wheel of the combination, and the combination dial has only to be turned back to the original number for the safe to open again. Business owners like this, since unauthorized employees cannot open the safe, yet the entire combination does not have to be redialed every time the safe is opened. Many businessmen forget about this completely, and occasionally leave their safes on day-lock even at night, and this affords yet another opportunity for an enterprising thief. Day-lock is exploited by turning the dial to the left as far as it goes before any resistance is felt. This resistance is due to the drive pin on the wheel being turned, coming into contact with the drive pin of the next wheel. At that point, the dial should be turned no more to the left. Now, the dial is turned to the right, one number at a time, with the handle tried at each number. If the safe is indeed on day-lock, the handle will give at the proper combination number, and the safe will open. If, however, the dial is turned to the right until resistance is felt again, the safe combination must have been completely scrambled after closing.

Surveillance certainly has its place in combination deduction, also. Basically, there are three types of surveillance possible: long range, video, or close range. At long range, one attempts, through binoculars or a telescope, to see the combination dialed. This assumes, of course, that one can spy the safe in question from a concealed place. Even if one cannot discern the exact combination, one may be able to see what neighborhood each number is in, thus lowering the possible combinations if one chooses to trial-and-error it. Video surveillance requires a remote control or timed video camera which attempts to capture the combination dialing on film for later viewing. The camera is, of course, disguised, and one must devise pretexts for planting and retrieving it. The third example of surveillance is close range, where one hopes not to see the entire combination dialed, but rather just the last number. This happens in small banks or businesses where the safe or vault is kept open during business hours, and the number on the dial is plainly visible. If the number on the dial remains the same for a long period, it is more than likely the last number of the combination sequence. One may ask what good one number of a three number combination is, but with just one number, a burglar can trial-and-error the other two in just one weekend. This trial-and-error trick was accomplished on a six combination vault in the film *Honor Among Thieves*, which was supposedly based on a true story. In addition, if one knows the make of the safe, one can plug that number into the try-out combination formula used by the manufacturer (see Appendix A).

Another trick to learn a safe's combination is to first knock the combination dial off of the safe or otherwise mess it up, then plant a bug in the room the safe is in, to listen in on the conversation while the locksmith fixes it. Chances are, the combination will be discussed during his visit.

Before moving ahead to manipulation, there are a couple more ways of combination deduction to discuss. These methods are rather fantastic, and I lend little credence to their success, but they are included here for the sake of completeness. One doubtful technique is the tape-recorder trick. Supposedly, one can place a disguised tape recorder in someone's not-too-quiet safe, and upon retrieval, the tape speed is slowed and the volume amplified to produce a series of "clicks." These clicks are then counted to deduce the combination. Assuming a tape recorder can capture the precise number of clicks, how does one know from where the safe-opener began dialing, or where the combination dial changed direction? There are simply too many variables for this to be a reliable technique. And the same negative appraisal goes for hypnotism. Assuming one can hypnotize the manager of a bank under a pretext, that he knows the combination, and that he will not remember your asking him for it, it is generally agreed by professional psychologists that no one will do under hypnosis something they would never do while conscious. These last two tricks are interesting and fine for mystery novels and the movies, but I sincerely doubt their effectiveness in real life.

3

Manipulation Techniques

The art of manipulation has been around at least 100 years, for manipulation-proof locks were manufactured as early as 1910. This method of safe entry, however, was and has always been known only to a few highly-skilled locksmiths. Manipulation today is based largely on the techniques of Harry C. Miller, who developed a scientific approach to manipulation in the 1940's.

Manipulation is the safe opening trick you've seen countless times on television. Our hero sticks an ear to the safe, turns the dial a few times, and *voila*... the safe is open. Well, of course, it's not that easy in real life (thank goodness), but it is indeed possible. Locksmiths must practice manipulation a great deal to master it, and so too must a safecracker if he wishes to apply it successfully. If you wish to follow along with this chapter, and fully understand it, I suggest you get an old safe, or perhaps a mounted combination lock mechanism.

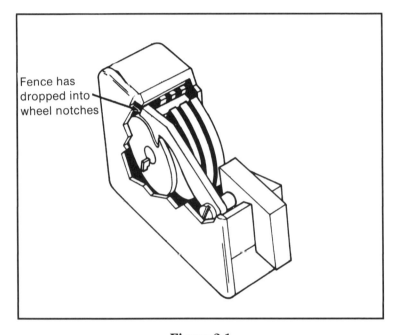

Figure 3-1

*When the proper combination is dialed, the lever
and fence fall into the notches of the wheels of the
wheel-pack, allowing the bolt to be retracted.*

As you'll remember from Chapter 1, when the proper
combination is dialed (see Figure 3-1), the lever and
fence fall into the notches, allowing the bolt to be
retracted, but when an improper combination is dialed,
the fence and lever simply rest upon the wheels. When
the sloped notch in the drive cam comes in contact with
the lever, it allows the lever to fall slightly into the notch.
This is called the *drop-in area*, and its discovery is the

first step in manipulation. To do so, rotate the dial at least four times to the left to pick up all the wheels. Continue turning left slowly until the nose of the lever drops into the drive cam gate slightly (see Figure 3-2).

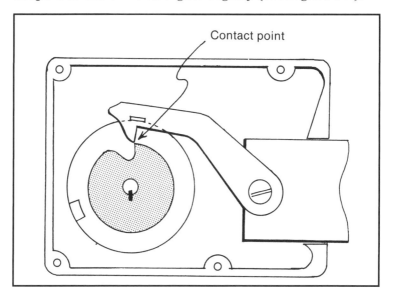

Contact point

Figure 3-2

In safe manipulation, the dial is turned to the left until the nose of the lever drops slightly into the drive cam gate. This is the first contact point.

Continue rotating the dial slowly to the left. The next indication will be the nose of the lever striking the right side of the drive cam gate (see Figure 3-3). These are called the *contact points*, (the space between them is called the *contact area*), and it is these points which will allow you to determine the combination.

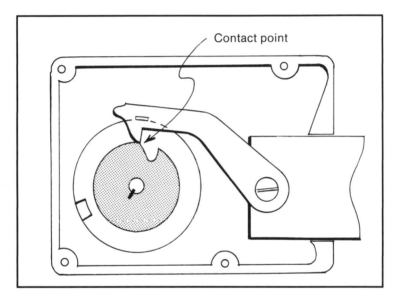

Figure 3-3

After finding the first contact point, the dial is turned to the left until the nose of the lever strikes the right side of the drive cam gate. This is the second contact point.

The second stage of the manipulation process is to determine the exact number of wheels in the lock. Turn the dial to the left at least four times to pick up all the wheels. We know the contact area — let's say, for example, it is between 10 and 20 on the combination dial. Continue to move the wheel-pack to the left, and park the wheels at a number far away, say 60, from the contact area. Now, turn the dial to the right, and as you pass 60 (or wherever you parked the wheels), you'll hear the drive pin come in contact with the fly of the first wheel. That's one. Continue rotating to the right, and every time at 60, you'll hear and feel another wheel being picked up. That's two. Continue this process, and when you hear no more fly contact at 60, you've run out of wheels. Most safes have three or four, but some have six, seven, eight, or more. For the sake of simplicity in this example, though, we will use a standard three wheel mechanism.

The third phase of manipulation is the actual charting of data taken from the combination dial. On a graph, such as the one shown in Figure 3-4, enter the left and right contact points in the appropriate boxes. Fill in the other boxes with the whole numbers nearest the contact points. We begin the graph by turning the dial right, four times around to pick up all the wheels. Continue right until the dial comes to "100" (or "0" on some safes), and park the wheel-pack there. Now, rotate the dial left to the contact area and take the left and right contact point readings. In our example graph (Figure 3-4), we see that our left contact point, 48⅛, was transferred to the graph by placing a dot on 48⅛ on the left "100" line. The right contact reading, 56¼, was transferred to the graph by placing a dot at 56¼ on the right "100" line. As you see, the graph goes in increments of three, so our next reading occurs at 97. Now, rotate the dial right again to "100" to pick up the entire wheel-pack, then park the wheels at 97. Now, rotate the dial left again to the contact area, and record left and right contact points on the graph, just as you did before. The new contact points in our example are 48½, and 56¼. These new points are now placed on the 97 line. This process is repeated until the entire graph is filled out. If you've taken accurate

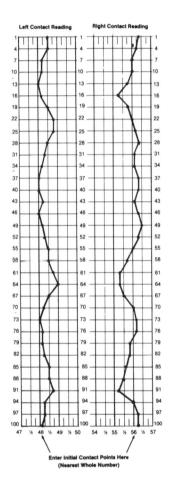

Figure 3-4

*The third phase of manipulation is charting
the data taken from the combination dial.*

measurements, your graph should look something like Figure 3-4, with three (or however many wheels you discovered in step two) sections of the lines converging on one another. The numbers where the lines approach each other are the numbers of the safe combination.

As you see, the lines approach one another in the upper-teens, the mid-sixties, and the lower-nineties. More often than not, it will be difficult to determine the exact combination with this graph, so an amplified graph must be done for each number, since this first graph reflects such broad allowances.

On the amplification graph of the first number (see Figure 3-5), the readings are taken every half number, instead of every three numbers, and the increment lines are adjusted to read ⅛ measurements instead of fourths. The rest of the process is done exactly as for the original graph. An amplification graph is done for each number, and the numbers of the combination will be found.

Since you don't know which wheel is indicating which number, you must try all possible combinations to find the proper sequence. With a three number combination, there are six possibilities. In other words, since the numbers from our amplification graphs would be 16, 63, and 92, we must try all of the following combinations: 16-63-92, 16-92-63, 63-16-92, 63-92-16, 92-16-63, and 92-63-16. One of these should be the proper combination. If the safe refuses to open with any of these attempts, it is possible that a slight error was made in the amplification graph, so you'll have to "bracket" each number slightly. Bracketing means that if your amplification graph gives you a number of 16, you should try 15 and 17, just to be sure.

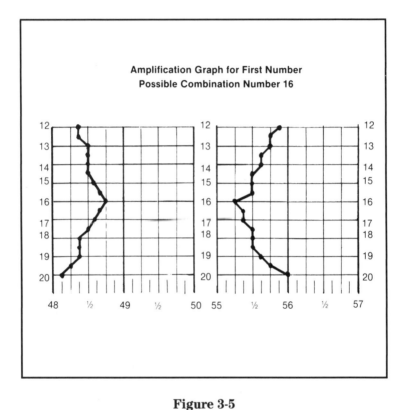

Figure 3-5

*The amplification graph for the first number gives
16 as a possible combination number.*

On newer safes, dials are extremely quiet and well balanced, making manipulation, which requires a lot of listening and feeling, much more difficult. To aid in manipulation, locksmiths and burglars alike use audio amplifiers which attach to the safe to detect tiny noises that would ordinarily go unnoticed. Many different types are available from locksmith suppliers, but just about any high-quality amplifier that is altered to attach (via magnet, suction cups, etc.) to a safe will probably suffice.

Some high-tech safecrackers eliminate the human element altogether, by using electronic sensing equipment (see Figure 3-6). This equipment is designed to

Courtesy: Wayne B. Yeager

Figure 3-6

Some high-tech safecrackers eliminate the human element by using electronic sensing equipment.

combine the sight and sound elements of manipulation, without the potential of human error. It consists of high-quality headphones for maximum sensitivity, specially designed filters to eliminate undesirable and irrelevant noises, and an electronic "memory" oscilloscope with a sound wave analyzer. The human ear is not sensitive enough to detect the different sounds which emanate from the lock, but when using this equipment, each "click" is illustrated on the oscilloscope as a wave. Since the memory function can be utilized to freeze-frame and compare various waves with similar characteristics, it is not too difficult for the user to calculate the combination by locating three or four identical wave patterns.

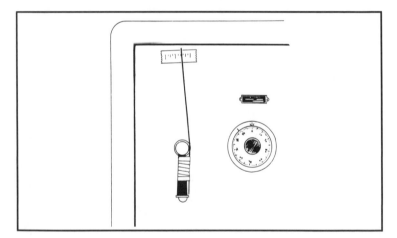

Figure 3-7

Some people use a "handle meter" for safe manipulation.
A long piece of stiff wire attached to the handle amplifies
the handle's movement so that it is easier to detect the
slight increase in handle movement when one of
the wheels is in the drop-in position.

Some people also design a "handle meter" for manipulation, since there is a slight increase in handle movement when one of the wheels is in *drop-in* position. This trick uses a long piece of stiff wire attached to the handle to amplify the handle's movement so that slight variations are more easily detected. The wire, at least 12″ long, is attached to the handle very securely. At the top of the wire, a calibrated card is placed on the safe so that the wire movements can be recorded more accurately (see Figure 3-7). The wheels are all turned to the left and brought to the contact area, or drop-in point. Note the position of the wire at this point before continuing. Now, turning the dial one number at a time, the handle is turned each time and a reading taken. When a wheel's notch is under the fence, indicating one of the numbers of the combination, the wire indicator will move ⅛″ or more on the card. Continue this process as in normal manipulation, until all of the wheels have indicated a combination number. This process, though sometimes used alone, is even more effective when used in conjunction with the previous manipulation methods.

I've also opened safes by vibration (see Figure 3-8). If a good-sized industrial vibrator (used in concrete settling) is applied to an inexpensive safe, the wheels will begin to spin slowly from the intense vibration. Sometimes, if a wheel spins its way under the fence, the fence will catch slightly on the notch of the wheel and trap it, so that it cannot spin further. By altering the directions of the vibrating force, it is possible to catch every one of the wheels in this manner. I suppose the reason that this hasn't become really popular among safecrackers is because industrial vibrators are terribly loud, and they numb your hands after holding them a few minutes.

Courtesy: Wayne B. Yeager

Figure 3-8

An industrial vibrator can be used to discover the combination of a safe.

Obviously, the various versions of manipulation are not techniques that are easily learned by reading about them. One must practice diligently if one is to master the intricacies of this exacting procedure. Although manipulation is sometimes difficult, anyone with perseverance can perform an opening with these techniques, if they adhere to the basic guidelines outlined here.

4

Safe Drilling Methods

Drilling is perhaps the most common method used by locksmiths to enter a locked safe, and is becoming increasingly popular with safecrackers as well. There are several different ways to drill a safe, all bringing about different results which ultimately lead to the safe's opening.

The first and most direct way to perform an opening is to drill for the locking lever or cam, and remove the obstruction that is causing the safe to remain closed. As shown in Figure 4-1, the tip of the cam cannot pass the locking bolt as long as the bolt is extended. In order to remove it, a hole is drilled as shown in Figure 4-2. Now the cam tip can either be partially removed by drilling chunks out of it, or moved out of the way by using a punch rod. The rod is used to bend the cam tip so that it passes on the other side of the locking bolt. It usually doesn't take a lot of bending to accomplish this bypass. The handles can then be turned to open the door.

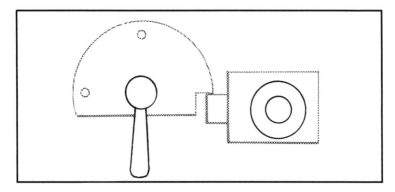

Figure 4-1

The tip of the cam cannot pass the locking bolt as long as the bolt is extended.

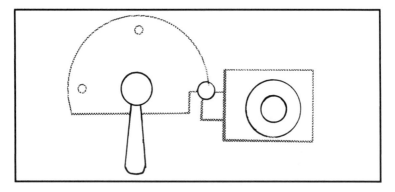

Figure 4-2

If the hole is drilled as shown, the cam tip can be partially removed, or moved out of the way.

The second method of drilling is not an attack on any safe mechanism itself, but rather it is a way to create a "peephole" into the wheel-pack. This type of drilling requires an intimate knowledge of safes, for one must know the proper angle and depth to drill. If seen from a side view (see Figure 4-3), the wheel-pack can be accessed

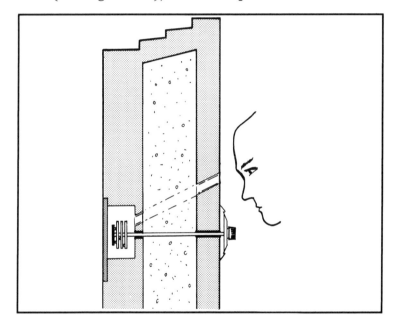

Figure 4-3

The wheel-pack can be accessed by drilling a small tunnel to it.

by drilling a small tunnel to it. Through this tunnel, a borescope (see Figure 4-4) is inserted. A borescope is a flexible, fiber-optic viewer that allows one to see into small holes or around corners. They are used in many professions, from medicine to engineering, and are avail-

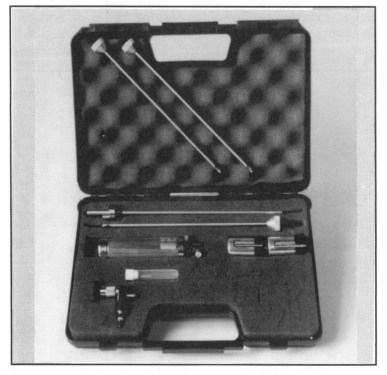

Courtesy: MDS, Inc.

Figure 4-4

A borescope is a flexible, fiber-optic viewer that allows one to see into small holes or around corners.

able from any locksmith or scientific supplier. With a borescope, one is allowed to see the wheel-pack (see

Figure 4-5), and one can then deduce the combination. This is done by recording the numbers seen on the dial when aligning the wheels, seen through the borescope. This set of numbers will not be the exact combination, but these numbers will be the same distance from one another as the numbers of the real combination. So, all one has to do is add 1 to all of the numbers until the right combination is found. Say, for example, that in order to perfectly align the wheels (as seen through the bore-scope), you had to dial 30-40-50. One then begins dialing 31-41-51, 32-42-52, etc., until the proper set of numbers is hit.

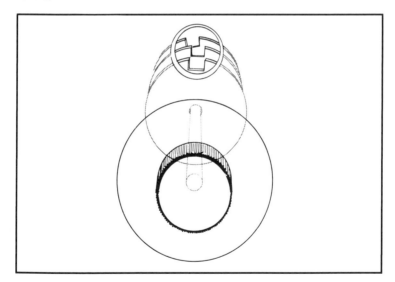

Figure 4-5

With a borescope inserted into the tunnel drilled to the wheel-pack, one can see when the wheels are aligned, and one can determine the correct combination.

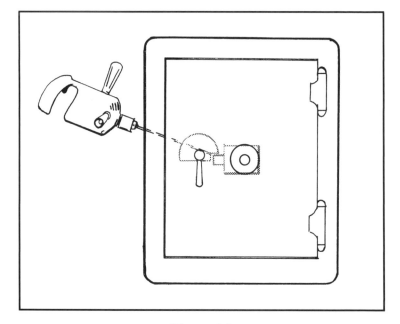

Figure 4-6

*In side drilling, a drill bit about 9 or 10 inches long
is used to drill from the side of the safe to the locking
bolt. The locking bolt can then be punched out of the
way allowing passage of the bolt cam.*

The third method of entry is side drilling. This method
requires a very long drill bit, about 9″ or 10″, to reach the
distance from the side of the safe to the locking bolt (see
Figure 4-6). The theory of this method is that by gaining
access to the locking bolt, one may punch it out of the
way to allow the passage of the bolt cam. Determining the

proper place to drill requires some knowledge of the safe encountered, but there are some general rules of thumb that can be applied. Draw an imaginary line from the center of the combination dial, and extend it around to the side of the safe about 3″ (see Figure 4-7). Drill here, while tilting the drill bit down slightly. A good, lighted borescope is needed here to penetrate the darkness, but once the bolt is located, a long punch rod replaces the borescope. The rod is then given a good punch with a hammer, so that the bolt is driven out of the way. The cam is now free to turn, so the handle will then open the safe door.

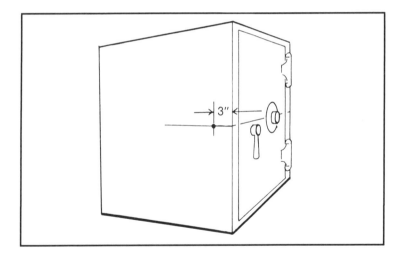

Figure 4-7

There is a general rule of thumb for finding the proper place to drill in side drilling. The safecracker draws an imaginary line from the center of the combination dial, and extends it around to the side of the safe about three inches.

The fourth method of drilling is an attack on the handle shaft itself. The plan here is to drill directly through the center of the handle shaft to shear off the threads of the attaching screw, which permits access to the cam.

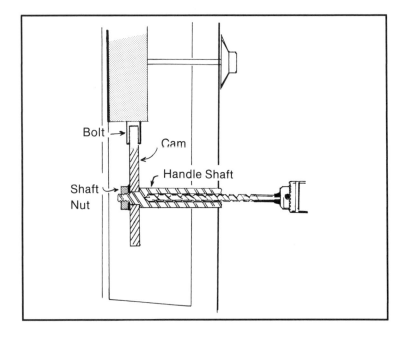

Figure 4-8

If a safecracker drills through the center of the handle shaft,
all the way through the shaft, he will drill off the thread at
the end of the handle and the attaching nut will fall off.
This allows him to remove the handle shaft completely.

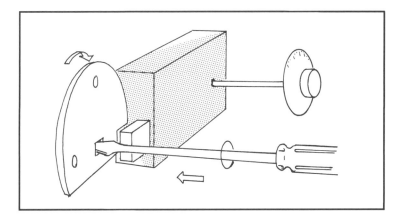

Figure 4-9

After removing the handle shaft, the safecracker inserts a large screwdriver into the square hole in the center of the cam, and presses firmly. This moves the cam under the bolt and allows the cam to be bypassed. The door can then be opened.

The usual method of approach is to first cut the handle off as close to the door as possible, so that the handle shaft can be seen. The exact center of the shaft is marked, and a long ⅛″ bit is used to drill a leader hole all the way through the shaft. A larger bit, about ⅜″, is then used to follow this hole to the end of the shaft (see Figure 4-8). If the hole is straight and accurate, you will have drilled off the thread at the end of the handle, and the attaching nut will fall off. This will permit you to remove the handle shaft completely. With the shaft gone, a large screwdriver is inserted into the square hole in the center of the cam (see Figure 4-9), and pressed firmly while turned in the opening position. As the inward pressure is applied, the cam will be moved in under the bolt to allow the bypass of the cam. The door will then open.

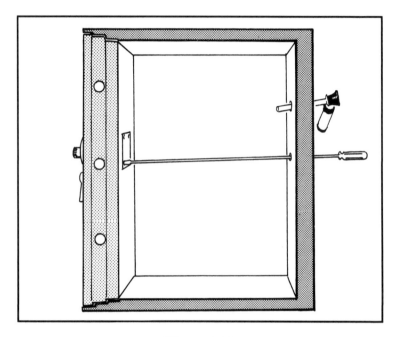

Figure 4-10

*A safe man can drill two holes into the back of the safe,
one for a borescope, and the other for the insertion
of a long screwdriver.*

Another area of a safe that is vulnerable to a drilling attack is the back. Two holes are drilled into the safe interior (see Figure 4-10). One hole is for a borescope, and the other is for the insertion of a long screwdriver. The safe man removes the screws on the back of the wheel cluster so that a portion of the wheel cluster is now visible. Using the special screwdriver, the wheels can be turned and the bolt retracted.

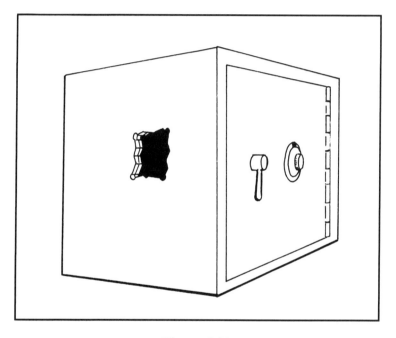

Figure 4-11

A safecracker can drill a series of holes to create a 4" x 4" square. This square can then be punched out with a sledgehammer, allowing a hand to reach in and remove the contents of the safe.

One final trick of the safecracker is to drill a square of holes (see Figure 4-11), and punch this square out with a sledgehammer or cut it out with a cutting torch. After making this small hole, he then reaches inside the safe to remove the contents. Crude, but effective.

Well, now that you know the methods and purposes of safe drilling, we should discuss the actual mechanics of the drilling process. Any area vulnerable to a drilling attack, such as the door, sides, or back, will most likely contain, in the higher security models, a plate of hardened steel. The placement of this hardened steel varies from safe to safe, but you'll know it when you hit it. Plates vary in thickness from ⅛″ to ⅜″, but most are about ¼″ thick. This steel is usually hardened to 62-64 on the Rockwell scale, and requires a carbide, tungsten, or cobalt-tipped drill bit (see Figure 4-12) to penetrate it. Drilling hard

Courtesy: Strong Arm Security, Inc.

Figure 4-12

To penetrate a hardened steel safe, a carbide, tungsten, or cobalt-tipped drill bit is necessary.

steel requires a great amount of steady pressure, and plenty of drill bits. A freshly sharpened ⅜″ bit will cut efficiently for only about two minutes, and it often takes up to ten to penetrate the plate. A strong individual who can maintain a steady pressure should use a drilling speed of about 2000 RPM, but a smaller person should consider a higher speed of about 5000 RPM. The higher the drill speed, the smaller the drill bit required, and the less pressure needed to penetrate the hardened steel.

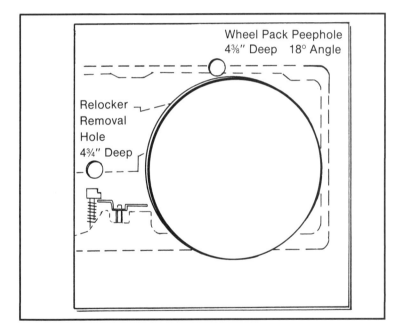

Figure 4-13

*A drilling template is available for just
about every make and model of safe.*

Another factor one must consider is the angle at which the safe is to be drilled. This depends upon the physical construction of the safe itself, and is adjusted for the minimum amount of work. Such information is best obtained by a working knowledge of safes, or by using drilling templates. A drilling template (see Figure 4-13) is available for just about every make and model of safe. All a safe man must do is place the template against the safe, and he has an instant x-ray view of the contents. Using this, he has no trouble in deciding exactly how to drill. There is caution taken in the distributing of safe drilling templates, so the safecracker most often has to use the trial-and-error method. As you can see in Figure 4-14, the

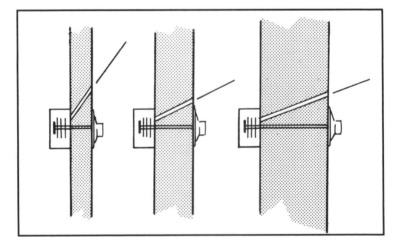

Figure 4-14

*The proper angle of drilling depends
on the thickness of the safe door.*

thickness of the door determines the proper drilling angle. It is rather hard to know how thick a safe is by looking at it, but 15° is a good starting angle when door drilling.

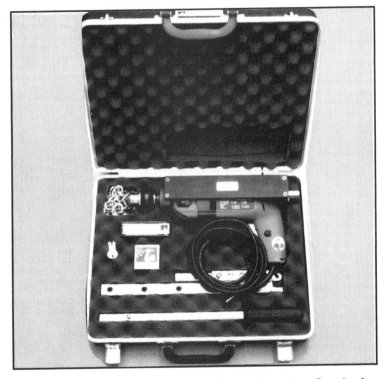

Courtesy: Strong Arm Security, Inc.

Figure 4-15

*A drilling rig is a portable drill press which attaches
to the safe itself and allows much more control and
drilling pressure than free-hand drilling.*

One problem with safe drilling is that one must drill very accurate holes at sometimes precise angles, under difficult circumstances. Framon Manufacturing Co., Strong Arm Security Co., and others, have come to the rescue with their various drilling rigs. These devices, which attach to the safe itself, are portable drill presses which allow much more control and drilling pressure than free-hand drilling.

Now that we've seen the purpose and mechanics of safe drilling, it is obvious that drilling is quite an effective and efficient means of safe entry. It is also much neater than the methods that follow.

5
Punching and Peeling

Punching and peeling, more violent methods of safe opening, are very popular means of attack among safecrackers when facing older or cheaper safes.

Peeling, or stripping as it is sometime called, entails de-laminating a safe by prying up a corner, and removing sheet after sheet of metal like a multi-layered can of sardines. One uses a crowbar, axe, or steel wedge to pry an edge at the upper right hand corner of the safe, near the door. One layer after another is peeled until the interior of the safe is reached. With models made prior to 1960, this can be quite successful at times, although it takes a great deal of time and effort.

The primary tools of peeling are very crude, and include the ax, pick, crowbar, steel wedges, bolt-cutters, and sometimes an electric jackhammer. In a few minutes, a burglar can inflict an incredible amount of damage to a safe with these tools.

Many years ago, safe manufacturers began replacing the relatively thin steel faceplate with thicker metal, and started using cement-like lining under this metal. This slowed the burglar down, but cheaper safes and fire safes are still particularly susceptible to this type of attack. New high-quality safes, however, have seamless one-piece bodies which defeat any attempts at peeling.

In punching, the theory is to force the cam out of the way of the lock bolt, so that the door will open. This is accomplished by knocking the combination dial off the safe, and using a strong punch rod to forcefully knock the spindle into the cam. This will, on older model safes, force the cam out of the way of the lock bolt, allowing the handle to turn and the door to open. Modern safes have effectively removed this opportunity, however, by using relocking devices which engage during a punching attempt, plus many have spindles of lead or other malleable, soft metal which spreads out on impact rather than moving the cam.

6

Torches, Etc.

Since any metal can be melted at a hot enough temperature, even the toughest safes lend themselves to various methods of burning. One way to accomplish this is by torch, and the other is by incendiary.

One type of torch is the oxy-acetylene variety, capable of temperatures between 4000° and 4500° F in the hands of a skilled operator. At this temperature, an oxy-acetylene torch is a very effective tool for cutting most steel materials, but has some difficulty in piercing thick, hardened steel plate. Another type of torch, the thermic lance, or burning bar, is used extensively in the construction industry and can reach temperatures of over 7000° F. In the hands of an expert, the lance will penetrate the most advanced safe construction in the world, if given enough time.

Usually, cutting is accompanied by other methods of safe opening, such as drilling or the use of explosives. However, cutting itself is often used if one needs only to make a hand hole large enough to retrieve the safe's contents, or remove enough metal to reach the internal lock mechanisms. Cutting with an oxy-acetylene torch is quickly becoming out-dated as safe manufacturers are graduating to harder, high-tech alloys, but is still effective in opening older and less expensive safes.

The thermic lance has become the weapon of choice for most advanced safe burners, and for good reason. Its incredible heat will penetrate a six-inch thick block of tempered steel in 15 seconds. The lance is actually a hollow iron pipe packed with a combination of high-carbon steel and magnesium rods, which burn and act as a flux to remove the molten metal. Burglars who use a thermic lance simply cut themselves a new door in the safe or vault, and grab the loot. Because of the drawbacks of using a thermic lance, such as the need to wear a special fire suit, the dense quantities of smoke produced, and the bulk of the equipment, a new, smaller version, called the Keri-Coil, was produced.

The Keri-Coil is essentially a miniature version of the thermic lance, and is used extensively in underwater metal-cutting. It uses a 40-foot long flexible steel cable which replaces the rods of the burning bar. The Keri-Coil is portable and easy to conceal, and will, I feel, become a very popular burglary tool in years to come.

Thermite, a mixture of iron and aluminum flakes, is also a very useful tool in the burglar's arsenal. When ignited, (which is difficult and must be done with a small torch) it burns at an incredible temperature, and quite literally turns hardened steel plate into bubbly, molten metal in seconds. If placed on a safe, it will melt the metal almost instantaneously, allowing a metal punch or long screwdriver to be poked through. Recipes for thermite and other incendiaries are given in Kurt Saxon's *Poor Man's James Bond*. Gas masks are usually worn when using thermite, for it gives off noxious fumes when burning.

Although it seems safe burning is an easy way to gain entry, there are many drawbacks for the would-be safecracker. First, in order to create a temperature hot enough to cut the safe's metal walls, the temperature inside the safe (even with insulation) may reach a point hot enough to burn the contents. Paper currency ignites at about 500° F, and this poses a problem for those using this type of heat. Most burglars, once a hole has been pierced into the safe, pour water into it to protect any money or other important objects from burning.

Torches and thermite also create a lot of noise and huge quantities of smoke, which is likely to set off any burglar or fire alarms nearby. (See *Techniques of Burglar Alarm Bypassing* for information on this subject.)

7

Explosives

One of the burglar's favorite methods of safe entry is via high explosive. Nitroglycerine is still widely used today, but the power, reliability, and safety of plastic explosives, such as C-4, is favored by modern safe-crackers over the Old Timers' "grease."

Back in the old days, nitroglycerine was simply drained from dynamite sticks, but when stricter guidelines for dynamite manufacture were introduced, burglars found it necessary to make their own. Nitro is simply a mixture of Nitric and Sulfuric acids with a little glycerine thrown in. There are several books on the market today which offer the recipe, but one of the best is Uncle Fester's *Home Workshop Explosives*.

When blowing a safe with nitroglycerine, the safe-cracker also needs a moldable substance to create a funnel-like device. Historically, soap (such as Fels

Naptha) has been used for this function. When the soap is hand-kneaded for about 15 minutes, it becomes a very malleable substance with a consistency that will not permit the nitro to leak through it. Also in the safe-cracker's tool bag should be a strip of cellophane, blasting caps, and a prybar.

Of all nitroglycerine techniques, the most common is what is called the "jam-shot." It is feasible on most safes, round and square door alike, and requires no physical movement of the safe. The purpose of the jam-shot is to blow the door open while still on its hinges. Occasionally a safecracker will use too much "grease" and blow the door completely off, or not enough "grease," which requires either another shot of nitro, or some serious door-prying.

The piece of cellophane is folded into an 8"x ½" strip, and placed lengthwise into the space between the door and the door frame. The soap is fashioned into a cup, with a funnel shape made around the cellophane. This must be a tight fit, so that the nitroglycerine will not dribble down the front of the safe door. When the cup and funnel is finished, the cellophane is carefully pulled out, with pains taken not to jar the soap funnel. This provides a channel for the flow of the nitroglycerine once it is introduced into the cup. The blasting cap is placed carefully into the cup, and the wires are unrolled and extended to the battery hookup, which should be safely out of the way of the explosion.

The nitro is now poured into the cup, and the safe-cracker observes the rate at which the safe is "drinking." Nitro is a syrupy liquid, and there must be a continuous, unbroken chain of liquid all the way to the detonator. When approximately one ounce has been consumed, and the burglar has determined that a continuous river of nitro exists from the last drop down inside the door, all the way to the blasting cap, he sets off the detonator. This is the real art of safe blowing — knowing exactly when to detonate. If all goes well, the safe door will be blown open, and the contents revealed.

The "gut-shot" or "spindle-shot" is another very popular nitroglycerine method. The use of the gut-shot is limited, though, since the safe must be moveable, and the modern safe's relocking device (see Chapter 10) may render this technique useless.

The gut-shot requires that the burglar first knock off the combination dial with a hammer, then tilt the safe over on its back. A blasting cap is attached to the spindle, and an eyedropper-and-a-half of "grease" is allowed to trickle down the shaft of the spindle. The nitro will find its way into the locking mechanism, and when detonated, will destroy the entire "guts" of the lock. The door can then be opened by simply turning the handle.

In addition to nitroglycerine, professional burglars use castable high explosives such as C-4, PETN, RDX, or TNT to either blow a hole in the safe, or blow the safe apart. These high explosives can sometimes be purchased from legitimate users, or can be manufactured using a formula in *Home Workshop Explosives*.

The ribbon charge is simply a rectangular box of high explosive placed on or near the target safe (see Figure 7-1). To help direct the force of the explosion, several bags filled with water are placed on the charge. This also serves to significantly reduce the noise level of the explosion. This type of explosive technique will usually penetrate 3-4 inches of steel, so obviously a great amount of damage is done to the safe. Under certain circumstances, shaped charges may be used to blow a safe. These are much more efficient since they have a predetermined direction of force, but a situation where they may be used effectively is often difficult to contrive.

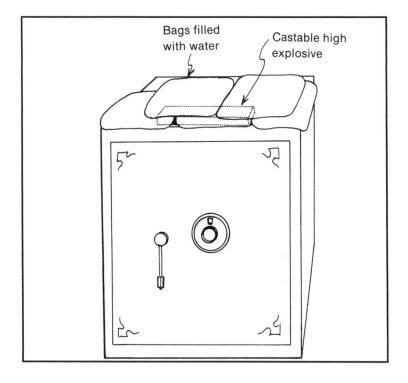

Figure 7-1

A ribbon charge is a rectangular box of high explosive placed on or near the safe.

Another popular trick among safe blowers, is to drill a small hole into the top of the safe, and fill it with butane, propane, or other highly combustible gas. A stopper made of modelling clay is placed over the hole, and a fuse is inserted. When the gas is ignited, the force of the resulting explosion may be enough to demolish the safe, I've even heard of one obviously amateur burglar who actually filled a safe with gasoline, and lit it. Not only did it blow the door off, but it destroyed the entire safe, the contents, and very nearly the safecracker as well. These techniques would obviously be worthwhile only if the safe's contents could not be burned.

Finally, a new and ingenious method of safe blowing is being seen more and more frequently these days. Again, a burglar drills a small hole into the top of the safe, and fills it completely with water. Then, a pencil-shaped section of C-4 or other moldable high explosive is inserted in to the hole. As you know, water does not compress, so when you detonate the explosive in this setup, the safe is usually obliterated (with the contents more or less intact).

Several recent technological advances in safe design and manufacture have curtailed the use of explosives by some burglars, but professional safecrackers don't see mechanical improvements as a real threat. Any safe can be beaten with explosives; it is the time and noise factors that actually catch criminals.

8
Miscellaneous Methods of Safe Entry

I've decided to lump all the other common methods of safe entry into this one chapter, since most of these can be fully described in a paragraph.

One of the most common tricks to defeat small safes is to simply remove it and work on it elsewhere, with a little more safety and privacy. Fire safes, small money chests, and even wall safes can be pushed, pulled, or rolled to the burglar's vehicle. If burglars can find a way to attach it, a winch is sometimes used to remove large floor safes and wall safes. Also, if a safe is located on an upper floor of a tall building, it may be dropped to the pavement, in hopes that the impact will jar the door open. (If this sounds kind of silly, you should know that Underwriters' Laboratories tests new safes for protection against this.) But if the safe doesn't bust open, the thieves will try to make off with it somehow.

A relatively new method of safe opening is by using radiological equipment. The operator positions the device in such a way that he is able to see a real-time x-ray of the working parts. He has only to dial the combination by watching the wheels line up under the fence. This method has not yet been exploited by burglars, as far as I know, but if it ever begins to gain popularity, safe manufacturers will simply install a sheet of lead in front of the locking mechanism to prevent this from being accomplished on all new safes.

Figure 8-1

Safes with digital keypads are gaining popularity.
To open such a safe, one has only to press
several numbers consecutively.

Safes with digital keypads (see Figure 8-1), instead of combination dials, are gaining popularity these days. In order to open a safe with a digital keypad, one has only to press several numbers consecutively instead of dialing a combination. The handle is then turned to allow the safe to open. Therefore, if the burglar knows the proper buttons to press, he can enter the safe just as easily as the owner.

To discover these numbers, a burglar will often apply invisible Ultra-Violet ink to something that the legitimate safe opener must touch (door knobs, handrails, etc.) prior to his opening the safe. When he then presses the buttons, some residual UV ink will invariably stick to them. The burglar then has only to place an Ultra-Violet lamp near the keypad to discover which buttons were pressed. A variation on this trick is to use a detective's fingerprint kit. Once the keypad is dusted, it should be easy to tell which buttons are pressed, by observing the latent fingerprints.

Some safecrackers also attempt to "grind" an opening by using a gasoline powered concrete saw (see Figure 8-2). I suppose this may work with cheaper fire safes, or when one needs to remove an outer layer, but the use of this high-speed abrasive wheel would probably be totally ineffective against hardened steel plates.

Although you don't hear of it much in America, the use of acids still remains a major threat in other parts of the world. The crook with various acids, and an expert knowledge of their use, can do incredible damage to safes which contain normal alloys. Some safe manufacturers have experimented with various combinations of metals to curb this attack, but acid is still highly effective if given enough time. I suspect, though, that the use of acids as a safe attack will remain relatively rare, for they usually do more damage to the inexperienced safecracker than they do to the safe.

Figure 8-2

Some safecrackers use a gasoline powered concrete saw to "grind" an opening.

9

Safe Deposit Boxes

Once inside the safe or vault, the safecracker may encounter either a "keister," a miniaturized inner safe, or safe deposit boxes. The small internal safe is defeated with the same techniques given throughout this book, but the safe deposit box requires a different approach.

The typical modern safe deposit box (see Figure 9-2) consists of two keyways, one for the guard key, and the other for the customer's key. So two different keys are required to open each box. The insertion and turning of the two keys cause a bolt to retract, allowing the box to open on its hinges.

The most common method used by amateur thieves to perform an opening is sheer physical force. By using a crowbar, sledgehammer, steel wedges, and other tools, a safe deposit box will eventually yield. This, however, is loud, slow, and not guaranteed, so most advanced burglars prefer to use a nose puller (see Figure 9-3). A nose puller uses a threaded machine screw to actually pull out the cores of both lock mechanisms. A screwdriver can then be inserted in the holes to turn the cam and release the bolt. This is fast, quiet, and effective.

Courtesy: Mosler Safe Co.

Figure 9-1

The American Pac2 Mini-Vault from the Mosler Safe Co. contains safe deposit boxes.

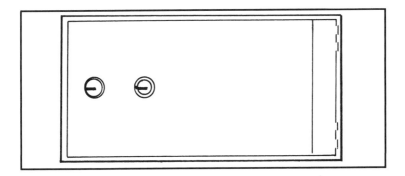

Figure 9-2

*The typical safe deposit box has two keyways, one for
the guard key, and the other for the customer's key.*

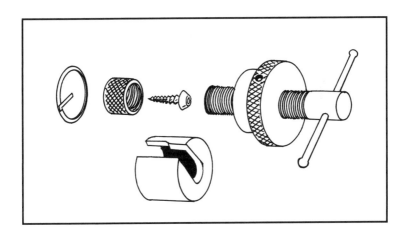

Figure 9-3

*To open a safe deposit box, most advanced
burglars use a nose puller.*

There is also the hinge method of attack. The first step in opening safe deposit boxes with the hinge method is to break a portion of the hinge (see Figure 9-4) with a sharp ½" steel chisel. Notice in the illustration that the box is designed to retain the door, even if this happens.

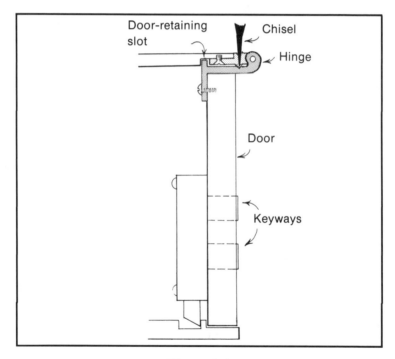

Figure 9-4

The first step in opening a safe deposit box with the hinge method is to break a portion of the hinge with a sharp ½ inch steel chisel.

Therefore, a wedge shaped chisel is used to spread the door hinge out of the retaining slot. A few hard raps with a hammer will cause the door to snap in (see Figure 9-5). This trick is very quick and easy, but can be used only on boxes with exposed hinges.

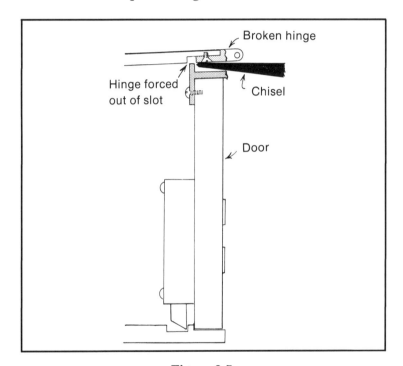

Figure 9-5

A few hard raps on the butt end of the chisel with a hammer will cause the door to snap in.

The most common method of opening used by locksmiths is drilling with templates. Templates are available for just about every model of safe deposit box currently used. Below is an example of a fairly common template. It is placed against the box itself, and one knows immediately where one must drill to open it. The locksmith usually attacks the hinge screws so that the door may be removed completely. Note also that the template has a drilling location for a sight hole, which would allow the locksmith to actually see the tumblers. He could then raise the individual tumblers to their necessary heights, so that the gate will pass, allowing the bolt to retract. This isn't difficult to do with practice, and does not harm the safe deposit box at all. In fact, once the hole is plugged, it's as good as new.

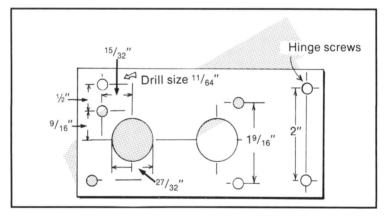

Figure 9-6

*Locksmiths most commonly open safe deposit boxes by
drilling with templates. A template is placed against
the box itself and the locksmith immediately knows
where he must drill to open it.*

10

Deterrence and Prevention

The first line of defense for safe owners is to deny the safecracker access to the safe itself. This is accomplished by hiding wall safes behind paintings (as seen hundreds of times in the movies), disguising a safe as an end-table, hiding floor-mounted safes under rugs or flooring, or submerging them in steel-reinforced concrete. Also to prevent anyone from obtaining the combination by long-distance surveillance, many lock and safe manufacturers have started using spy-proof dials (see Figure 10-1).

The second line of defense is to equip safes and vaults with alarm mechanisms, so that even if the safe is discovered, it cannot be tampered with. One of the most popular safe alarms is the proximity sensor. It is attached to the safe itself, making the safe one giant sensor. It detects the presence of the electrostatic charge inherent in every human body, and is sometimes sensitive

Courtesy: Schwab Safe Co.

Figure 10-1

To prevent anyone from obtaining the combination by long-distance surveillance, many safe manufacturers have started using spy-proof dials. (See also Figure 10-1a on next page.)

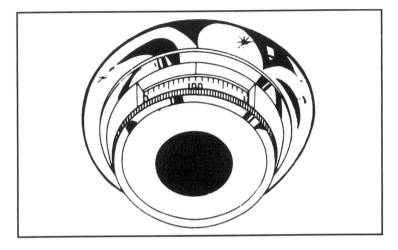

Figure 10-1a

enough to detect an intruder at four to five feet. Safes and vaults may also contain a magnetic switch on the door, to alert someone when the door is opened, or they may contain a Passive Infra-Red sensor that detects motion once the safe door is open. To learn how burglars overcome these devices, read *Techniques of Burglar Alarm By-Passing*, available from the publisher of this book.

Some safes and most vaults rely on a Time-Lock mechanism to protect the contents during non-business hours. When the time-lock is set, the safe can be attacked with the methods previously described, but will not open (in theory) until the prescribed time has elapsed. Safe-crackers have found that time-locks, which are usually attached to the inside of the door, can be overridden by tilting or dropping the safe, or by attacking the doors and sides with a 20 pound sledgehammer. These repeated blows are often enough to off-balance the tiny, precision components of the timing mechanism. UL also tests for this on many of the new vaults, and many of the time-locks fail during this test.

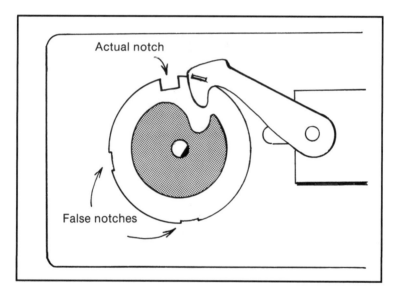

Figure 10-2

Many safe manufacturers cut false notches into the wheels. This slows down safecrackers opening safes by manipulation.

As you remember from Chapter 3, manipulation is made possible because one can detect the changes that occur when the notch of a wheel comes under the fence. To slow this process, many safe manufacturers cut false notches into the wheels, so that one does not know if one has detected a real notch or a fake one (see Figure 10-2). These manipulation-resistant wheels do slow the process down considerably, but a safecracker with time and perseverance can still perform an opening. In addition to the false notches, new safes have a very quiet wheel-pack, and it is next to impossible to manipulate these without electronic amplification.

If a burglar attempts to knock the combination dial off, and punch the spindle, he may be in for quite a surprise. Several safes now contain (and many people are requesting locksmiths to install) a glass vial of tear-gas just behind the spindle. If the spindle is punched into this glass vial, the tube will break and release a large quantity of strong, irritating vapor. I don't think this method of prevention is extremely effective, for the safecracker who plans to punch a safe can simply wear a gas mask to avoid any potential fumes. If the spindle is punched, and no tear-gas appears, he could safely remove the mask. This would certainly deter only the amateur safecracker.

Speaking of fumes, some high-security safes, which risk an expert attack by a thermic lance, have chemicals embedded in the barrier material which emit a nasty smoke when burned. This smoke, however, must conform to federal guidelines, and cannot be in any way toxic. Therefore, this smoke is simply a minor nuisance, for the safecracker who uses a thermic lance is, more than likely, already in an asbestos helmet. Also, safes which risk thermic lance attack almost always contain a sheet of copper or other good heat conductor at vulnerable cutting points. This copper sheet spreads the thermic lance's heat so quickly that the barrier material beneath it receives only a fraction of the actual heat output. As in most other attempts at deterrence, this is more of a delay than a protection device, for the copper can only withstand 7000° F for so long.

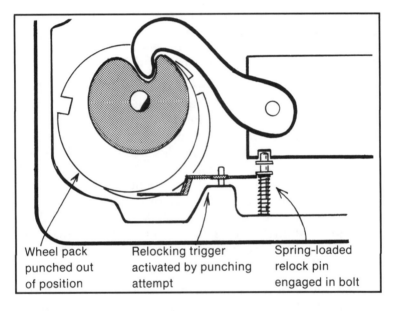

Wheel pack	Relocking trigger	Spring-loaded
punched out	activated by punching	relock pin
of position	attempt	engaged in bolt

Figure 10-3

Most safe combination locks have some sort of relocking device which keeps the bolt from being retracted should anyone try to get inside the safe. The relocker has a trigger which must be tripped before the relocker engages.

Most manufacturers of safe combination locks have implemented some sort of relocking device in the locking apparatus. The relock mechanism serves to keep the bolt from being retracted should one try to punch the spindle, detonate explosives, or physically attack the safe in any way. The relocker has a trigger which must be tripped before the relocker engages (see Figure 10-3). About the only way to defeat a relocking device is to drill to it, and move it from its holding position. This spring-loaded lever can be pushed away from the locking bolt with ease; the only real problem is getting to it. The location of the relocker varies from safe to safe, so templates are indispensable for determining these exact locations.

Drilling attempts are now occasionally frustrated by ball bearings, which some manufacturers embed in the safe-wall material. When a drill bit hits a ball bearing, it has a tendency to roll off, rather than penetrate it. A steady drilling rig alleviates this problem somewhat, but burglars often find it necessary to incorporate other devices, such as torches or chisels, into their plan of attack as well.

If you have a safe that is of inferior quality, or was manufactured before 1940, you should consider having a professional locksmith upgrade it a little. For around $50, he can make some alterations to the locking mechanism, lengthen the bolt, and generally modernize the safe a bit. As this will greatly increase the chances of outlasting an amateur attack, this is money well spent. Also, theft insurance is a very worthwhile investment for businesses that handle a lot of cash. If you live in a small town, don't make the mistake of thinking that a weak safe is strong enough to protect against any attack from the amateur locals. It may very well be, but there are gangs of expert safecrackers that roam the country, and they actually prefer small town Mom and Pop stores.

As we've seen, there are far too many points of vulnerability for any safe or vault to be labeled "absolutely secure." And, as history shows us, what is difficult to defeat today will eventually become child's play for the professional safecracker. As the saying goes, anything man can create, he can destroy. With safes, it just takes a little longer.

Appendix A
Manufacturers'
Try-Out
Combinations

The combinations listed here were set by the manufacturers at the factory, and were intended to be changed
by the new owners. Many people do not know this, or do
not bother to change them, so these combinations will
open a surprising number of safes in operation today.
The combinations listed here are preceded by a coded
dialing guide, such as R4L3R2L. This means that if a combination is given as 10-20-30, one must turn the dial
RIGHT FOUR turns, stopping at 10, then LEFT THREE
turns, stopping at 20, then RIGHT TWO turns, stopping
at 30, then LEFT until the wheel-pack stops.

American Safe Co.

R4L3R2L

30-20-10	10-20-30
40-10-50	30-20-10

Cary Safe Co.

L4R3L2R

40-60-35	56-13-36
50-86-32	10-60-35

Chicago Safe Co.

R4L3R2L1

7-8-2-1	35-71-39-7

R5L4R3L2

40-70-60-30	40-50-60-70	40-50-67-70
30-60-40-70	40-30-60-70	50-30-70-60

Diebold Safe Co.

L4R3L2R

45-70-35	60-20-40	35-70-45	70-30-55
40-20-60	17-37-62	67-27-47	22-44-88
11-22-44	18-36-72	45-35-70	90-70-35

Mosler Safe Co.

L5R4L3R2L
64-95-60-5   91-39-76-59

L4R3L2R
50-15-80   25-15-30   45-52-50   50-40-50

R5L4R3L2R
15-30-45-65   20-40-60-80

L4R3L2R1
36-39-43-87   40-20-60-88   20-40-60-80

L4R3L2R1
9-4-3-2   25-60-45-5   5-25-45-60
40-20-60-30   20-40-60-30   40-30-60-20

Meilink Safe Co.

L3R2L1R
2-34-10   0-34-10   0-36-12   0-38-14   0-40-16   0-42-18
4-36-12   2-36-12   2-38-14   2-40-16   2-42-18   2-44-20
6-38-14   4-38-14   4-40-16   4-42-18   4-44-20   4-46-22
8-40-16   6-40-16   6-42-18   6-44-20   6-46-22   6-48-24
10-42-18   8-42-18   8-44-20   8-46-22   8-48-24   8-0-26
etc.
(each digit increases by two until 48, where it begins at 0)

Schwab Safe Co.

L4R3L2R

15-75-0   75-50-0   40-70-35   35-75-45   65-35-45

Victor Safe Co.

R4L3L2R

0-12-82-92 1-13-89-93 2-14-84-94 3-15-85-95 4-16-86-96
5-17-87-97 6-18-88-98 7-19-89-99 8-20-90-0 9-21-91-1
10-22-92-2 11-23-93-3 12-24-94-4 13-25-95-5 14-26-96-6
15-27-97-7 16-28-98-8 17-29-99-9 18-30-0-10 19-31-1-11
etc.

(each number increases by 5, until 99, where it begins at 0)

Appendix B
Suppliers of Lock and Safe Opening Equipment

C.O.L. Manufacturing
7748 W. Addison
Chicago, IL 60634

Thermic Lance manufacturer

Foley-Belsaw
6301 Equitable Road
Kansas City, MO 64141

Sells various safe-opening tools and books, also nose puller

HPC, Inc.
Schiller Park, IL 60176

General locksmith supply, some safe tools

Lockmasters, Inc.
5085 Danville Road
Nicholasville, KY 40356
Sells safe-opening videocassettes and training packages

MDS, Inc.
1640 Central Avenue
St. Petersburg, FL 33712
Manufacturer of special safe-opening borescope system

Safeman Supply
1104 NE 126th Avenue
Vancouver, WA 98684
Sells drilling templates for most safes

San Diego Safe Co.
PO Box 9795
San Diego, CA 92109
More drilling templates

Strong Arm Security, Inc.
2228 Kenry Way
So. San Francisco, CA 94080
Safe drilling bits and drilling rigs

The Locksmith Store
1229 E. Algonquin Road Unit E
Arlington Heights, IL 60005
General locksmith supplier

Selected Bibliography

Letkemann, Peter. *Crime as Work.*. Englewood Cliffs, N.J: Prentice-Hall, 1973.

Wright, W.J. *Safe and Vault Manual*. Detroit: M.H. Jaf Co., 1948.

Professional High-Tech Burglary. Iron Press, 1988.

French, Scott. *B and E: A to Z, How to Get in Anywhere, Anytime*. Videocassette. Boulder, CO: CEP, Inc.

Kenton, Bill. *The Complete Story of Safe Deposit Locks*. Self-Published.

Safeman's Guide. Volumes 1-10. Park Ridge, IL: Locksmith Publishing Co., 1970-1989.

Technique of Safe and Vault Manipulation. Cornville, AZ: Desert Publications, 1975.

McOmie, Dave. *National Locksmith Guide to Safe Opening.* Streamwood, IL: The National Publishing Co., 1987.

Fester, Uncle. *Home Workshop Explosives.* Port Townsend, WA: Loompanics Unlimited, 1990.

Saxon, Kurt. *The Poor Man's James Bond.* El Dorado, AR: Desert Publications, 1972.

Yeager, Wayne B. *Techniques of Burglar Alarm Bypassing.* Port Townsend, WA: Loompanics Unlimited, 1990.

YOU WILL ALSO WANT TO READ:

☐ **52032 THE COMPLETE GUIDE TO LOCK PICKING,** *by eddie the Wire.* This is the single finest treatise on lock picking ever printed — over five years of research went into its preparation. Detailed, illustrated, step-by-step instructions are given for picking all the commonly found lock types. Also covered are various other ways of bypassing locks, how to mount practice locks, and much more. *1981, 5½ x 8½, 80 pp, profusely illustrated, soft cover.* **$14.95.**

☐ **52050 TECHNIQUES OF BURGLAR ALARM BYPASSING,** *by Wayne B. Yeager.* Any alarm system can be beaten. This book shows how. Dozens of security systems are described in illustrated detail: Magnetic Switches; Window foil; Sound and heat detectors; Photoelectric alarms; Central Station Systems; Closed circuit TV; And much more. You'll learn how they work and how they can be defeated. A must book for anyone concerned with security. *1990, 5½ x 8½, 104 pp, illustrated, soft cover.* **$14.95.**

☐ **52047 THE B & E BOOK: Burglary Techniques and Investigation,** *by Burt Rapp.* A practical manual designed for the police officer in charge of a burglary investigation and civilians interested in reducing their vulnerability to theft. Includes: Illustrated Breaking and Entering Techniques; Getaway; Safecracking; Fencing Operations; Gathering Evidence; A Guide to the Best Tools and Equipment. This book tells you everything you need to know to investigate and prevent burglaries. *1989, 5½ x 8½, 149 pp, illustrated, soft cover.* **$16.95.**

☐ **10052 CODE MAKING AND CODE BREAKING,** *by Jack Luger.* We live in an information age: information is bought, sold and stolen like any other good. Businesses and individuals are learning to keep their secrets safe with this practical, illustrated guide to building and busting codes. Learn how to construct simple and complex codes. Learn how computers are used to make and break codes. Learn why the most unbreakable code isn't always the best. Ideal for those interested in professional and personal privacy. *1990, 5½ x 8½, 125 pp, illustrated, soft cover.* **$12.95.**

••

Loompanics Unlimited
PO Box 1197
Port Townsend, WA 98368

SAF8

Please send me the books I have checked above. I have enclosed $_____ which includes $4.95 for shipping and handling of the first $25 ordered. Please include $1 more for each additional $25 ordered.. Washington residents include 7.9% sales tax.

Name _____

Address _____

City/State/Zip _____

Now accepting VISA and MasterCard. 1-800-380-2230 for credit card orders
***only.* Monday through Friday, 8am to 4pm PST.**
Check out our Web site at: www.loompanics.com